STEP BY STEP ON HOW TO MAKE MONEY ONLINE

(extra bonus: become an Ebay Powerseller in just months)

M.MONTT

Disclaimer:

Neither the author nor the publisher will be responsible for the use or misuse of the information contained herein. The information contained in this book is for information purposes only. It is not intended as professional advice or a recommendation to act. Before engaging in any activity mentioned in this book, seek the advice and consultation of a competent professional, and only act upon that counsel.

Although the best efforts have been undertaken to ensure the information contained herein is accurate, neither the author nor the publisher makes any such warranties as to that accuracy.

There are some companies and/or websites that are mentioned in this book, but only for the purpose of providing additional information to aid you in your own research. Neither the author nor the publisher endorses any of them, or makes any official claims on their behalf.

In any entrepreneurial endeavor, there is the risk of loss. Any suggestions of how much money can be made in any activity listed in this book should be considered strictly anecdotal and atypical. The actual amount that you might make may be more or less, including a net loss of capital. Please research any moneymaking plan that you might be considering with the same due diligence that you'd apply to any potential business activity.

All trademarks mentioned herein are the property of their respective trademark owners.

Legal Notice:

While all attempts have been made to verify information provided in this publication, neither the Author nor the Publisher assumes any responsibility for errors, omissions, or contrary interpretation of the subject matter herein.

This publication is not intended for use as a source of legal or accounting advice. The Publisher wants to stress that the information contained herein may be subject to varying state and/or local laws or regulations. All users are advised to retain competent counsel to determine what state and/or local laws or regulations may apply to the user's particular business.

The Purchaser or Reader of this publication assumes responsibility for the use of these materials and information. Adherence to all applicable laws and regulations, federal, state, and local, governing professional licensing, business practices, advertising, and all other aspects of doing business in the United States or any other jurisdiction is the sole responsibility of the Purchaser or Reader.

The Author and Publisher assume no responsibility or liability whatsoever on the behalf of any Purchaser or Reader of these materials. Any perceived slights of specific people or organizations are unintentional.

Contents

Introduction

The Secret Ingredients to a successful online business

   The Law of Financial Growth

   What's Your Passion?

   A Money-Making Niche

   The 3% Who Succeed

What type of online business do you want to Start?

   Membership Sites

   Writing Your Own eBook

   Affiliate Products

   Online eBook Store

   Creating Your Own Membership Site 101

   Starting your own Membership Site

   Create an eBook that Generates Passive Income

   Make money with drop shipping

   Secrets to become a Powerseller in just a few months

Final Words

Introduction

I know you probably don't believe me when I tell you I make thousands just by sitting at my computer.

As amazing as it sounds, I actually do it regularly and it only consumes a few hours a day at my computer. And I really believe that anyone with a brain and a little persistence can follow my work and do exactly what I'm doing. I know a few secrets and I'm about to reveal them to you in the pages ahead. So keep reading if making thousands of dollars a month, a week, and even thousands of dollars a day sounds good to you.

Of course I won't guarantee that you'll make the same number of dollars I make everyday, but what I can do is tell you how I do it. I'll reveal some of my most hush-hush secrets, along with a complete money-making system that produces you some serious income!

"So, How Much Money Do You Have in Mind?"

After you finish reading this, you'll know every undisclosed secret I use to produce this income and you'll know how to do it the same way I do.

But keep in mind, you might not need a million dollars a year to support your lifestyle. As individuals, all of our income needs are different. It's possible that you aren't as materialistic as I am and it's possible you don't desire the expensive trips, cars, and homes. Heck, $1,000.00 a week might sound great to you especially if you don't want to work very hard and you don't need all the fancy stuff. I've even talked with some "Stay-at-home-moms" that say they'd be delighted to make just a mere hundred dollars a day if it meant they still got to stay at home and play with their kids all day.

Whether you want $100.00 a day or $1220.00 a day, this book is going to show you how your computer can help you do it!

I also think you'll be glad to know that I'm not a "Lucky" person and luck plays no part in how I make money. This is not some fluke that just worked one time for one person. On the contrary, the same system I'm about to show you is being used by hundreds if not thousands of other successful internet marketers that work out of their homes.

Yes, my particular approach is a little better than most, and it's definitely unique, but the basic nuts and bolts of my system have been making lots of other people serious cash for many years.

I've been working out of a small bedroom in my house for over two years. I have a small desk with a $700 computer sitting on it. There's nothing special about me, my equipment, or where I do my work. Many people that know me actually tell me I'm a cheap-skate in a lot of ways! I don't want a fancy office with a pretty secretary. I've seen too many big shots with offices, secretaries, and staff go broke. Fancy offices and pretty secretaries don't make money! On the other hand, the correct knowledge does make money. I'm just an average guy who happened to find out a few secrets that actually work! And you're just moments away from finding out how I did it.

As you read these secrets up ahead, you'll find out why you're never going to have to put much of your profits into overhead or business expenses. There's absolutely no reason for you to go out and get an office. Your home will work just fine unless your business grows too large to contain in your home. And that's a great problem to have!

You'll never need to have a bunch of employees. Employees are more trouble than they're worth with all the baggage they bring to your business.

One of the perks of working from your home is the fact that it doesn't matter what you wear while you're working. I work in my pajamas, robes, old torn sweats and holy jeans most of the time. Heck, you could answer the phone naked and your customers would never know. Your customers never come to your home and you never go to their home and since you never see each other in person, it's a relaxed atmosphere.

I actually get a lot more accomplished than I ever did working in an office because I'm so comfortable working in my house. There's no reason you can't do the same thing I'm doing. It's a piece of cake!

Now I'd like to tell you how I put this whole business system together and why it's going to be even easier for you than it was for me. I know you may feel like skipping ahead, but you'll be hurting yourself if you do. This system must be read in the exact order in which it was written for it to make perfect sense. It's important for you to know exactly each step I took. This system will make perfect sense if you see how it all began.

I'm about to show you what I do and how easy it's going to be for you to do the exact same thing in your home. And remember, the big checks I deposit in the bank are not some strange fluke and I didn't just get lucky. I just followed an exact method that guaranteed my success. It's really no different than when you use a recipe to make a delicious dinner. You just follow the recipe and add the exact ingredients. And you always get the same delicious meal.

You could also compare this to a restaurant chain like Burger King, McDonalds, KFC, Round Table Pizza, Carl's Jr., Taco Bell etc. Does the food taste different at a Taco Bell in California than it does at a Taco Bell in New York? No, of course not because they both use the exact same ingredients for every item on the menu. A Big Mac from a McDonalds in the United States tastes the same as it does in a McDonalds over in Europe!

Just understanding why all these restaurant chains are so popular and so successful is going to help you understand exactly how this system is going to make you successful.

What is the single most important common denominator all these restaurant chains have in common? Answer: Each one of these restaurant chains uses duplication to achieve their stunning success. The owners of these restaurants know that success can be achieved over and over again and again by simply following a set of instructions or reading a manual that contains the ingredients to a perfect recipe! Yes, duplication is the key!

The reason people who read this book become successful is because it contains the exact ingredients that have already made thousands of other people successful. So as you continue to read through this book, I want you to stop worrying, doubting, and over-thinking. I want you to treat the rest of this book just like you would treat any other great recipe that was recommended to you by a good friend. Remove any doubt you may have about this working for you and just know that you are following a perfect recipe that has always delivered success to everyone that has used these ingredients the way they are written below.

And just so you know, I still don't have an office and I have no desire for an office. I'm writing this book right this very moment from a spare bedroom in my house that I turned into an office. I'm living proof that one room in your home with one computer is all you need to make thousands of dollars! Most people dream about making this kind of serious money with a home business but many people don't make a single dime. It's still hard to believe that this little book you're reading right now has all the "ingredients" and the system to help you bring freedom to your life!

For so many years I tried business opportunities that just didn't work! I felt like a complete sucker because I kept buying every "Get-Rich-Quick-Scheme" I could find. I was addicted to buying money-making-systems. I've joined every MLM (multi-level marketing) scheme out there. I bought every "Work At Home" magazine and I responded to every ad. I ordered every course, program, system, and money-making report I could get my hands on. I ordered seminars on tape, franchises, distributorships, plans, and anything else that looked like it could make me stinking rich.

I spent $30 on one report and $99 on another. I spent $200 on a set of audio tapes and I spent nearly $400 on a distributorship. Heck I even spent $2,000.00 on a website that guaranteed I would make $600.00 a day! It never made me a nickel! In fact none of that stuff ever made me a penny!

I'd be ashamed to even tell you how many thousands of dollars I've spent on worthless get-rich-quick schemes. I bet you've had some similar experiences and you're now probably thinking the "Work At Home Dream" doesn't exist. If you're like I was, you probably don't know who to trust anymore.

I was there too! I remember how it felt to spend all my money and get nothing back in return. But I now realize that all those thousands of dollars I spent searching for a high paying business opportunity were not wasted! It's now clear to me that If I hadn't spent all that money trying different things, I never would have learned some of the secrets I'm about to share with you.

So why am I sharing this information with you? Well, here's the truth. I feel very fortunate. This system has given so much to me that I feel like it's now time to give something back. I remember how hard it was and what a struggle it was before I knew these secrets. And even though I had to spend thousands of dollars to find out one good piece of information that would change my life, I can only hope nobody else has to go through that long, difficult process. I don't believe anyone should have to go through that kind of stress and frustration. I now feel obligated to share my knowledge with you. Keeping these secrets to myself would be a selfish thing to do.

Anyway, it's not like it hurts me by telling you my confidential secrets. Some people have asked me this question: "Aren't you just creating more competition by telling all these people the secrets to your success?"

The answer is "No" and you'll find out why as you continue reading further.

Let's talk about what this book is NOT. First things first, I know some of you reading this right now still can't help but to be a little bit skeptical and have doubts about whether this system will really work for you. But just for a moment allow yourself to be open and receptive so you can truly take in this information and fully absorb it. I'll start by telling you what this system is not about.

It's not MLM, Multi-Level-Marketing, or Network Marketing. This system has nothing to do with that stuff. Don't get me wrong, I've actually made some money with MLM but I just think most people never find success with MLM and I have learned a much easier way to make money. And with this system, you never have to meet with anyone face-to-face and you never have to do any real selling. This system always sells itself so you just collect the checks! Since most of the work is automated in this system, you'll only need to sit at your computer for about an hour a day!

This system is not one of those pyramid schemes that doesn't even have a "Real" product. No Way! With this system, all of the money you're going to make will come from providing "Real" products with a legitimate purpose to people who are desperately seeking them. And they'll always pay you top dollar for your product! Every time! I'll give you more information about your product in the next few pages, but I just want you to know that I don't just sit around selling "Get-Rich-Quick" information. No way, there's probably good money to be made doing that, but that's just not what I do.

My goal is to see you become completely independent. Your goal in obtaining this system was to learn how to become financially free and completely independent so you don't ever need to rely on others for a paycheck. And most important, you don't want some fat cat boss-man taking most of the money for the work you do in life.

I did not make this system up. I'm sure you've seen the get-rich magazine ads and infomercials that show the owner of the company standing next to a Mercedes, next to their giant cruise ship, or even standing on the stairs of their own leer jet. And you probably already know that many of the people posing in those pictures aren't even the real owner of the company. Often times the person in the photo-ad has a completely different name than the one you see advertised. Yes, these guys often use made up stage names and they set up their own photo shoots showing a life of luxury when it's not even real. All fake!

I want you to know strait up that I'm nothing like that fake stuff you see out there. No way, I'm a real person and if you saw me walking down the street you'd see me as a regular person. I don't act like the rich and I don't look like the rich. I look completely ordinary, dress completely ordinary, and even drive ordinary cars. I don't need to impress anyone. In fact I rather go out of my way to look like regular folks because I don't want to be treated different in life.

You'll soon see that even a 10 year old child could use this system (where was this when I was a kid). You don't need much money to start up. So even if you're almost broke, there's still plenty of hope. You don't need any special education. You don't even need an office or a store to do this. You don't need to stock any inventory of products and you don't need any special equipment. Best of all, you don't need to have a single employee working for you, ever!

Be prepared to fully understand the big picture. Because once you fully understand what I'm talking about, you're never going to work for anyone else again. You're money worries will be gone forever, and I promise you this: The people that work in your bank will soon have a new respect for you and know you on a first name basis.

But first, let me tell you my story. For nearly a year I tried every internet money-making opportunity I could get my hands on. But I just kept racking up more debt. Six months later, I was in some major debt and desperately struggling. Any sane person would have gone out and gotten a job. But to me, a job was not an option. So I just sat at my computer all day long and I answered as many of those "opportunity ads" you see in the back of small business magazines as I could find. I tried every money-making scheme that I came across. If you sold a get-rich-quick scheme, I would have been an easy sale for you at that time.

I tried offline businesses as well as online businesses, but they always turned out to be nothing but lies. And I kept falling for every one of them. It was official. I was an opportunity junkie. If there was such a thing as opportunity junkies anonymous, I probably needed to be there.

Remember, I'm not a lucky person and what I was about to discover wasn't luck. I discovered a recipe for success. Yes siree, I had found the exact ingredients for a serious cash income!

I was determined to find a way to get my computer to make me a solid income from home. That was my dream and I was obsessed with being my own boss and finding a simple way to make money from home. I wanted to be totally independent and financially free to relax at home where I felt safe. Looking back I sometimes can't believe that I never gave up and at least got a part time job to help get me out of my financial mess. But I guess I was well aware that every minute I spent working for a boss making low wages, was time wasted. I knew that having a boss and a job would only end up robbing precious hours from me and take away the time I needed to get my own thing going at home.

No boss! No cubicle, No office! I take orders from nobody! I am suddenly in charge of my own life! I can suddenly do what I want when I want without asking anyone! I can take the next month off for a tropical vacation half way around the world if that's what I decide to do.

How???

Let me describe what it was like in the moments leading up to my huge "Work At Home", "Cash Breakthrough" and discovery. I knew I was close and I knew I had already solved most of this money-making puzzle. Yes, I had so many pieces of this elusive puzzle already in place that I was starting to smell victory. But I was still missing one last piece of the puzzle and that one thing would finally make everything come together.

I thought I had read every book, course and system written by every marketing genius in the history of America, but I guess I was wrong. I was wrong because I found a "work-at-home" course on the net that contained the final piece of the mystery of "How to make a serious income working at home with a computer," written by a top internet guru.

You see, before reading about this "work-at-home" course, the most I've ever made on the internet was a measley $28.52. Obviously that's not even close to enough money to support yourself or your family, let alone buy yourself a steak dinner at the Sizzler.

But immediately after I read what this internet guru had to say, it explained the missing pieces of the puzzle, the ingredients. My income raged like a wild fire in high dry wind.

The Secret Ingredients to A Successful Online Business

Below I'm going to list off the main ingredients of my system that I learned from my own testing.

- The Law of Financial Growth

- What's Your Passion?

- A Money-Making Niche

- The 3% Who Succeed

Now, let's take a closer look at each of these key ingredients above and go over them, one by one. Keep in mind, you're not expected to understand how they all come together at this point. As we move forward, I'll begin explaining how each of them work.

Understanding the Law of Financial Growth

First things first, if you want to make your first million, you need to make your first hundred. You just can't make a million bucks if you do not know how to make your first hundred, or even your first dollar online, for that matter. You want to run? Learn how to walk first.

Focus on your first couple of dollars, online. Once you've made the a few bucks, then focus on making your first hundred. Then your first thousand, so on and so forth. Until, BLAM! Before you know it, you're sitting on a million bucks.

You read all those websites and books claiming they made thousands of dollars in one day, week, or month. That reads like eye candy, but it didn't happen overnight my friend. It won't. It took a lot of preparation to get to where I am today.

What's Your Passion?

I almost always hear someone ask, "How do I start an online business? What should I sell online and what products should I sell?" I always recommend that before you start, you need to determine your niche. Your niche is a topic about which you are, or can be passionate about.

Simply, if you don't love what you do, it's almost a sure bet that you won't prosper as much as when you follow your heart and do what you love to do. A typical mistake made by internet newbies is to try and market a product they know nothing about to a group of people they also know nothing about.

Those lacking in experience cannot make honest recommendations, and it shows in low sales and poor conversion rates.

There is an old saying, "Do what you love and the money will follow," which seems to hold true on the internet.

Choosing a Money-Making Niche

One of the biggest secrets that makes this whole thing come together is carefully choosing a niche market. But almost every marketer on the internet is fixated on selling a broad product with wide public appeal. And that's why 98% of all internet marketers are failing at what they're doing. There's a famous saying that all great marketers fully know and understand and it goes like this: "When you try to sell everything to everybody, you end up selling nothing to nobody." Another one goes like this: "When everyone's your market then no one's your market."

Why is this? Well, the simple answer is that it costs a lot more money to advertise to that broad audience we call the masses, than it does to advertise to a small niche market. Yes, you get a much better deal on advertising when you sell to a niche market.

The most common method people use to decide which niche market to get involved in is to simply ask yourself what your hobbies are? Or ask yourself what is of most interest to you in life? What fascinates you? This is often a niche market that you already know and understand. You may even be an expert on a niche market that you didn't realize was a niche. Are you? Think about the things you spend your spare time with.

The best thing about dealing with niche markets is the fact that they're so easy to manage. What I mean is that instead of trying to reach 300 million people that mostly don't care about your product, niches allow you to focus on around 20,000 prospects at a time. For instance, in a spy software business, there's only about 25,000 people that are subscribers to spy magazines. This means instead of trying to get lucky advertising to 300,000 people, I can now go directly to the 25,000 people that are most likely to become my customers. Kind of like shooting fish in a barrel when you think about it.

The 3% Who Succeed

Every day, thousands of people think about starting their own internet business. Some want to break away from the daily drudgery of working for someone else. Some need to supplement their main income. Some feel they are ready to expand their services beyond their circle of contacts. Still others…the list of personal reasons could go on and on.

But here's the catch… Everyday, most of these people do nothing but dream.

According to internet guru Ken Envoy, "The key to success on the Net for the small business owner is to master an in-demand niche." With a niche-focused business, your competition will be lower and it will be easier for targeted, interested visitors to find your website.

In the offline world, traffic is relatively easy to achieve – it's all about "location, location, location." However, in the online world, no one just happens to walk past, see your product or service and enter. Surfers on the net are not looking for you or your business. People search for information, for solutions. After all, if they knew you existed, they would not be searching. They would already be customers. Online, you must generate your own traffic to be successful. Your main task well before you make your first sale or contract to a customer, is to provide the information that people are searching for, in a way that the search engines like.

The secret of the 3% of small business owners who succeed on the net focus on…

"Information, information, information…"

By building a theme based content site, you will be growing your clientele from the ground up. Owning your traffic is essential to your longevity on the net because if you don't own your traffic, you don't own your business.

So, how did I build a website that made me thousands? It all boiled down to this do-able system:

1. Develop a valuable product or service – your own creation or someone else's.
2. Develop your own site in the niche that you know and love.
3. Fill that site with high-value content.
4. Use that content to attract your own niche-target traffic.
5. Build trust and credibility with all your visitors.
6. Use content that "presells" your targeted visitors. Then…
7. Convert "presold", willing-to-buy traffic into sales.
8. Diversify your revenue plan to include other monetization options

The process is simple and straightforward and easy once you shift your thinking to: Information first, income generation second.

You have to succeed at ALL steps. And the good news is that anyone can succeed if they combine motivation, the right process, and proper tools.

Building your web site can be quick, cheap and a simple process. It can also be a time-consuming, very expensive, and frustrating undertaking. It all depends on how much time, money and energy you are willing to spend

From doing it all yourself to having it all done for you, each option has advantages and disadvantages you should consider.

These are the 3 basic website building options:

- Do it Yourself
- Complete Website/eCommerce Package Deals
- Hire a Designer, Programmer, or Web Developer

Let's talk about "Doing it Yourself" and "Hiring a Designer".

-Do it Yourself: Building your own website is usually the least expensive option. On the other hand, the cost of building your own site can become very time consuming when you are new to the game. Also, it could become fairly pricey if you buy the most expensive graphic design programs and HTML editors. The easiest way would be to install Wordpress in your website, because is user friendly. Also, check out Youtube videos, where you can learn how to build your own website at no cost.

-Hiring a Website Designer: This could easily cost thousands of dollars to create 2 or 3 page mini sites. And also, there are no guarantees that you will be thrilled with the design.

-Get a Website Package Deal: If you are looking for a website building option that eliminates the need to learn HTML, use Site Build It! (SBI!) When you look at all the features that SBI! offers and start doing price comparisons, it's easy to see that you couldn't possibly buy all the components you need for an internet business site separately for the amount that SBI! Sells for.

Even if you could arrange domain registration, web hosting, auto-responders, html editors, etc…you still wouldn't enjoy the benefits of having all those utilities available through a single interface such as SBI! offers.

More importantly, you wouldn't be getting all the site research and analysis features that make SBI! The traffic building, sales generating machine that it is.

The SBI! eCommerce package will serve you well as you grow your business to include your own products. The Package includes:

- Domain Name Registration
- Web Site Hosting
- Site Topic Brainstorming and Researching
- Powerful Graphic tools (LogoCreator and NavBar Maker)
- Point and click site-building
- Easy web logging
- Search engine optimization
- Automatic search engine submission and re-submission
- Pay-per-click engine research and mass-bidding
- Traffic statistics and analysis
- Ezine subscription and delivery
- SpamCheck!
- Step-by-step Action Guide
- SBI! Newsletter
- The 4 Traffic Headquarters
- Tips 'n Techniques
- Link Exchange Assistance
- SBI! E-Goods

Site Build It! is the perfect option for someone who wants to save time and money by buying all the website building necessities in a neatly packaged bundle. If not, you can always find another website package that meets your needs. This is just what worked for me.

What type of online business do you want to Start?

There are many different ways to make money on the internet. Here are the 4 major ways to make money with information products:

1. *Membership Sites*

Membership sites are very popular right now. This is because instead of selling something once to a person, with a membership site you get that one person to buy from you every single month.

Membership sites are sites where you pay a certain amount (usually each month) to get access to information or services.

Here are a few examples of membership websites:

Information membership sites - Bmyers.com - Swepa.com

Services - Getresponse.com - Host4profit.com

2. *Writing Your Own eBook*

E-books always have and always be big sellers online no matter what anyone says. The fact that you can get information in your possession in a matter of minutes makes e-books a big winner over physical products.

Of course there are down sides to every business, and the e-book business is no different. The biggest complaint about e-books are the fact people are either A) buying them and asking for refunds or B) illegally giving away and selling the authors work without their consent.

But even though there are downsides, it is still more than worth it to sell your own e-book. Because the upsides greatly, and I do mean greatly outweigh the downsides.

To start, it costs virtually nothing to create e-books. All you need is to think of a hot subject, do some research and make that research into a book.

If you want more info on creating e-books, here are a few good resources:

http://www.7dayebook.com/

3. *Affiliate Products*

Affiliate businesses are probably the easiest to start, but also can be the hardest to make profitable. Simply because when you are an affiliate, you are promoting someone else's products.

So what are affiliate programs and how can you earn a constant monthly income with them?

Affiliate programs are a great way to get started marketing online. In essence affiliate programs or associate programs are revenue sharing arrangements where companies (merchants) pay webmasters commission for sending them customers.

In other words: You refer people to different websites that sell products. And if the people you refer buy, you get a commission.

Perhaps the biggest advantage of becoming an affiliate is that you do not need your own product! All you need is a way to send traffic to other people's websites and boom, you have started your own business!

Here is a guide that teaches you to do just that:

http://www.googlecash.com

You are paid a commission if the person buys a product or service, (Pay per Sale - Most Popular Option), clicks on an affiliate link (Pay Per Click - Less popular due to fraud) or simply fills out a form (Pay per Lead - Also Very Popular).

Basically affiliate programs are programs that enable you to sell other peoples products for a percentage of the sale. They are also a very hot topic at the moment.

You can virtually sell anything online now thanks to affiliate programs. If you want to learn more about starting your own affiliate business, you really need to read the following guides. http://www.clickbank.com.

4. *Online eBook Store*

An online e-book store is basically a website that sells e-books. While a conventional website usually sells only one e-book, an e-book store website sells many.

You can start an online e-book store 3 different ways:

-Write your own e-books and sell them in your online store website.

Since you will be creating your own products one-by-one, this will take a long time to set up.

- Buy resell rights to other people's e-books. This will be a lot faster than creating your own products, because you will be buying already made products.

However, you will need some start up money (probably about $1,000) to get this off the ground.

-Simply promote other people's e-books on your website. Basically, become an affiliate of other people's stuff by having affiliate links on your website.

5. *Creating Your Own Membership Site 101*

Want to sell subscriptions for online content with your own membership site? Selling online content via a password protected website has become big business. Not only is it fast to set up (with the right tools), but the start-up and running costs are minimal. Work from home entrepreneurs and big businesses alike are lapping up this new found revenue source.

People are willing to pay for online content. In fact, the "Online Publishers Association" revealed that pay-for content is emerging as a hot revenue model. Business content, personals/match making, and entertainment are the hottest niches. But even smaller niches, like DVD authoring, sports coaching, marketing services, and dieting are producing profits.

U.S. consumer spending for online content in the first 4 months of 2002 was $300 million, a growth of 155% over the first quarter of 2001 (and that's post-September 11th). It's apparent that online users will pay for content on their passion or profession. Subscribers are paying anywhere from $9.95 a month to $19.95, and in some cases up to $200 a month – depending on the nature of the content. Annual subscription renewals hold a solid 72%, giving site owners an impressive recurring residual income. Renewals accounted for nearly half of paid content sales in 2001. Less than 9% of online users currently pay for online content. This means the market is wide open for the savvy entrepreneur. Paying for content in 2002 was more than 5 times what it was in 2001. That's a massive 500% growth! Those who capture the market first in their niche will have the obvious advantage. It's an international market, so anyone can play.

6. *Starting your own Membership Site*

-Target the right market: Find a market that is passionate about a subject, and then build your membership site around it. There are so many topics to choose from. Doing a key word search will reveal what people are searching for online. You can know before you even launch a membership site if there's a big enough market.

-Make it unique: Ideally potential subscribers shouldn't be able to find the same information elsewhere for free online. Your job is to search online (and in some case offline) for content, and provide it in a convenient manner for your subscribers. Being unique could just mean having exclusive interviews with experts in your field.

If you've done the interview, then that's unique. Finding experts (and even famous people) to interview is not hard. In fact, as your site grows in popularity they are likely to contact you. This situation gives you a two-fold advantage. It gives you credibility or an endorsement, and it gives you exclusive content. Of course your exclusive content may be from your own specialized knowledge!

-Finding Subscribers: If you've started off targeting the right market, then finding traffic and subscribers aren't as difficult as some people believe.

-The best methods for generating quality traffic to your website include: Search engine positioning (including pay-per-click), Internet Joint Venture Marketing, Ezines (online newsletters), affiliate programs, and viral marketing (accelerated word of mouth marketing).

-Add tools or services: To enhance your membership site try including simple software, tools, ebooks, resources, etc. as a give-away. These can usually be found for free or at a very low cost online.

Giving people a reason to return to your members only area is critical – tools, resources, discussion forums and quality content will do that!

The exciting thing is, you can take your hobby, specialized knowledge or profession and turn it into a profitable membership site. Your challenge will be finding exclusive content.

You can start it part time – something I did myself, while working a full time job. As your subscriptions increase you can plan on full time involvement in your area of interest."

Starting and running a membership site can be a lot of fun and very fulfilling, however you need to know what's involved in setting one up, and then managing it effectively.

Planning and allowing for auto-responders, automated sign-ups, credit card processing, automated cancellations, etc is all part of a successful membership website.

As complex as this seems, many companies offer a low cost, easy-to-use software solution. A few companies, like MembershipSiteAdvisor.com offer a free software membership management tool to subscribers, allowing them to manage all of these routine tasks. This makes it possible for almost anyone to start and market a membership site for next to nothing.

The most important thing on your page is content. But don't worry, if you don't know how to write or you don't have the time to do it, you can pay for online content. You can find people to write for you for $5 in Fiverr.com, or if you want something more professional you can hire somebody at odesk.com.

7. Create an eBook that Generates Passive Income

Whether you like it or not, having your own product gives you more flexibility in your online advertising AND believe it or not, compiling an E-book is no more than a weeks work part time if done correctly and IF you do it this way the profits will come in for life.

Ok, lets get down to the nitty gritty. What is a viral marketing E-book and why should you create one?

A viral marketing E-book is a book which sole purpose is to be spread around the Internet quickly, by any means possible. It's not meant to make you money on the front end. You want other people selling it and giving it away to as many people as possible.

Why?

Because the inside of that book is full of affiliate links to other peoples products and every time someone gives away your book or sells it, (depending on how you want to do it) more people will be seeing your affiliate links, and this wont be costing you a penny!

So how do you go about creating your own viral marketing E-book? Here are the steps:

A good way to come up with ideas is to look at what others are already selling and mimic that.

You don't need to recreate the wheel here, so PLEASE don't make things harder then they have to be.

Get the tools you need to succeed. You are going to need a few tools here:

a) Domain name: You want a fairly short domain name that describes the content of your book fairly well. You can go to http://www.godaddy.com to register your domain name.

b) Web hosting: Let me say first, you get what you pay for. This has never been truer than with web hosting. YOU NEED a good reliable web hosting company with 24/7 technical support. If your site goes down and you can't contact anyone to help you get it back up, you will lose sales and a lot of them. I recommend you use http://www.bluehost.com or http://www.hostgator.com for the simple fact they offer all you need, plus a lot more for a reasonable price.

c) Autoresponder: You will need this so you can contact your prospects that don't purchase straight away. This is where you will give away your free course or someway to entice them to give you their email address so you can contact them periodically.

d) Credit card processor: Just use http://www.clickbank.com. This step is too easy. They will let you accept all major credit cards and start an affiliate program for a one time setup fee of under $50. They do take a percentage of every sale, but this is so much cheaper then getting your own merchant account.

Just about everyone selling E-books online is using Clickbank.com , you can also use paypal.com

e) E-book Software: You will more than likely want to create your book in PDF format so everyone can read it. Some E-books come in EXE format, but mac users can't read that format, so I find it best to use PDF. You can create your book with http://www.createpdf.com for a fairly cheap price.

f) Graphic Design Software: If you are anything like me, your artistic abilities peaked at age 7. So instead of busting my hump to create my E-book covers and website graphics I use sites like fiverr.com to get it done.

g) Outline your book chapters into articles: Writing a whole book in one sitting is hard, and trying to write a book without outlining the chapters is nearly impossible. My first book I ever wrote took me over 6 months but now most of my books take me less then a week to finish and that is with a sales letter and website up.

h) Write your content: Like I said just before, you need original content. There are too many books out there now where people are just regurgitating information others can get for free and this lowers the value of your book, which means less people will pass it around and even less will read it.

The best way to get a good amount of original information without writing it yourself is to interview experts in the field.

i) Create your sales letter: This is where you will be selling your book from and is critically crucial to your success.

Creating a sales letter takes a lot of work, especially if your new to the whole thing. The best way and the way I use, is to mimic successful sales letters.

If for some reason you think you can't do this by yourself, you have 2 options.

- Use software that helps put together your sales letter.

- Hire a copywriter

However, if you want to hire a professional copywriter, you are looking at thousands of dollars, plus royalties from your book sales.

Remember that you are selling this book with reprint rights, which means when they buy the book they can sell it as well. This is a huge selling point for you. You will also be giving them your Ebook cover, website graphics and sales letter.

j) Plug in your free 5 day autoresponder series: The best way to write your free 5 day course that your prospect get via your pop up window is to take chapters out of your book and put them in as a free teaser.

k) Advertise: Depending on your topic, you will want to target different people. However, no matter what topic you're selling on, there is one market who will want your book for the sole purpose of selling it, and that's the Internet Marketing group.

Your book could be on Hippo's but all they care about is the fact they can sell it as their own. This is why this type of book always does well. The key is to target people in your market and then the Internet Marketing crowd.

8. Make money with drop shipping

Have you ever wondered what makes an online buyer choose which store to purchase a product from, when there are various online stores selling the same products at different prices? There are a lot of factors that go into deciding where to purchase a product online- the most important being that the buyer is assured that they will receive their product with no hassle. Being that these are online stores, seller feedback based on costing, shipping, and communication is always important in discerning if one wants to engage in business with them. Still, many stores are reputable and it makes it even harder for a buyer to decide where to purchase. From a seller's point of view, these online competitors can cause some worry. This is where drop shipping can come in handy for a seller wanting to make more money and still keep their customers happy.

Drop shipping is an ingenious way to earn more money from selling products online. Basically, drop shipping is a term for selling products from a retail store setting into a wholesale store setting, but still at retail prices. In this way, the seller usually does not have many stocks of products on hand as they are coming from the wholesale market. Thus, there are fewer costs incurred on the part of the seller because the product is shipped directly to the buyer from the wholesale market.

For online sellers, the drop shipping method can be very appealing. It allows for sellers to offer a broader range of products without having to keep all of these stocks on hand, since the wholesalers have the products. This also means that inventory costs for the seller are decreased. Additionally, more variety in products also means a larger target market. Buyers are more likely to stick to one store that sells various items that appeal to them because it is more convenient, rather than to shop in one store for one item and then to a different store for another, thus being more time-consuming.

Whether you are just starting out with your online selling business, or already have a good grasp at online buyer-seller relationships, drop shipping can still be beneficial. There are training groups available in order to understand and learn more about drop shipping and how to effectively employ the method. [DS Domination](), established by Roger Langille, is a company that offers two types of training programs for people in different levels of understanding the drop shipping method. The DS Domination training program has different monthly fees for the various levels you choose to participate in, ranging from $19.95 to $99.95, but overall this program has helped many online sellers, like me, to make the most out of their ecommerce business and have higher profits.

Aside from training programs, DS Domination also helps online sellers benefit from drop shipping by providing optional affiliate programs and commissions on referrals. There are many testimonials from online sellers that give positive remarks about the DS Domination training program, showing that it has helped them increase their income on their own, and it gives them a sense of satisfaction knowing that their efforts on learning about the drop shipping method through DS Domination has been worthwhile.

If you are interested in making money drop shipping from Amazon to Ebay, here what you have to do.

Drop shipping method step by step:

1. First, search for an item (avoid electronics and books, too much competition) that is listed as PRIME on Amazon. Let's say you found a shoe rack. Now copy/paste the title of that item on Ebay and click search. If you find a picture like the one on the Amazon's page, is probably because that seller is drop shipping from them.

2. Click on the left side of your page, where it says "sold listings". If the item is listed on Amazon for $15.00 and you find a seller who sold it for $23.00, well he made almost $4 in profit (taking off the fees of Ebay and Pay Pal).

3. Repeat. Do the same, until you find a product that leaves a profit of at least $10.

4. Sign up for an Ebay account. List your item, copying the picture and description of Amazon's site.

5. The more you list, the better chances you make more money.

6. Once someone buys an item, you go to your Amazon account, buy that item and check on the box "as a gift" and ship it to your costumer.

Secrets to become a Powerseller in just a few months

1. Amazon's Prime: You must ship your items with prime. This way, your customer will receive the item real fast, and will give you positive feedback because of that. The more feedbacks you get, the more exposure you have on Ebay. But for this, you will have to create a new account every month. See, the free trial on prime memberships last for one month. Do that and create a new account every month. I use hotmail, because is very easy to set up a new account.

But, how do you manage to remember all those accounts? Well, you create a logic email address. For example, mysales1@hotmail.com, and then after the first month you go with mysales2@hotmail.com and so on.

Remember to cancel your free trial at the end of the month, or they will charge you $79.

2. Make more money: When you sell on Ebay through Amazon, many times you will see that the package is delayed or lost. When this happens, your eBay customer starts to get a little upset. But, you can turn around this situation to your favor! When something like this happens, just go to the Help section on amazon, and chat with them in the chatroom. Here is what you've got to say: "Hi, I'm a little upset because this order (and you put the order ID) is delayed or lost or whatever reason. Is there anyway you can make up with me for this? And most of the time they will give you a $5 or $10 dolars credit to your amazon account. In some cases they will offer you expedite shipping of that item. So, bottom line, any problem that you have with an amazon order you can make extra money, and when I say any, is any.

3. Look for amazon's deals: In the top of your page you click on Today's deals and then on coupons. Many times they will have $50 off some products. So, for example, a Phillips razor is 80 dlrs, with this coupon you get it for $30, so you undercut them on Ebay listing the item for $75 dlrs. You will sell like crazy this item!

Final Words

As you read this sentence, millions of people are making the kind of money you have always dreamt of on the internet.

This is your chance to join them. This is your chance to make your dreams come true and afford the kind of life you have always wanted.

I hope you realize the significance of the information you have been given in this "book" and I hope you put this newly found knowledge to good use.

The last thing I want to leave you with is this:

Could you turn $1000 into a million? No, but you could turn it into $2,000…

Could you turn $2,000 into a million? No, but you could turn it into $4,000…

Could you turn $4,000 into a million? No, but you could turn it into $8,000…

Could you turn $8,000 into a million? No, but you could turn it into $16,000…

Could you turn $16,000 into a million? No, but you could turn it into $32,000…

Could you turn $32,000 into a million? No, but you could turn it into $64,000…

Could you turn $64,000 into a million? No, but you could turn it into $128,000…

Could you turn $128,000 into a million? No, but you could turn it into $256,000…

Could you turn $256,000 into a million? No, but you could turn it into $512,000…

Could you turn $512,000 into a million? Yes, you can turn it into $1,024,000…

IT ONLY TAKES 10 STEPS TO TURN A THOUSAND INTO A MILLION…

GOOD LUCK!!

For more info visit www.homeincomefastnow.com

www.ingramcontent.com/pod-product-compliance
Lightning Source LLC
Chambersburg PA
CBHW081820170526
45167CB00008B/3484